W9-CAA-007

TEEN LIFE 411™

I'VE BEEN RACIALLY PROFILED.

NOW WHAT?

ALEXANDRA HANSON-HARDING

ROSEN
PUBLISHING®

New York

Published in 2015 by The Rosen Publishing Group, Inc.
29 East 21st Street, New York, NY 10010

Copyright © 2015 by The Rosen Publishing Group, Inc.

First Edition

Library of Congress Cataloging-in-Publication Data

Hanson-Harding, Alexandra.
I've been racially profiled. Now what?/Alexandra Hanson-Harding.
    pages cm.—(Teen life 411)
Includes bibliographical references and index.
ISBN 978-1-4777-7984-2 (library bound)
1. Racial profiling in law enforcement. 2. Discrimination in law enforcement. I. Title.
HV7936.R3H36 2015
363.2'308900973—dc23

        2014021036

Manufactured in China

CONTENTS

For some people living in the United States, the color of their skin can make others feel uncomfortable and, as a result, make them fearful about their safety and freedom.

You're thirteen, biking home from your friend's house, and suddenly you notice that a car is following you. At first you wonder: Is this for real? You make a turn toward your house and it's still crawling behind you. Your heart starts racing. Why are you being followed? You get home, and two plainclothes police officers get out. They tell you to put your hands up, handcuff you, and lean you against a cop car as more police show up. Meanwhile, your parents are being held back. Your neighbors are watching. You have to wait until the victim of a recent burglary shows up and says you weren't the burglar. Finally, the police uncuff you and leave—with barely an apology.

That's what happened to Martin Greenwell. His mother, Ava Greenwell, wrote an article for CNN about his experience. Greenwell says that what happened to Martin is one example of racial profiling. Why? When she listened to the 911 tapes, it turned out the police were on the lookout for a black male in cargo shorts who had committed burglary. No further description was given—or asked for. The description of a burglar including only his race and one item of clothing meant that way too many black males could be targeted.

Unfortunately, Martin's humiliating experience is all too common. What is racial profiling? It is when law enforcement officers rely on race, color, or ethnicity as the basis for investigating people as criminals. It can also extend to unequal treatment in the justice system. When people of a certain background are singled out for overly harsh school punishments or followed in stores by security guards, it is also racial profiling. Some people argue that "stand your ground" laws, which give individuals the right to shoot at people whom they feel threatened by, contribute to racial profiling.

Greenwell said "police officers . . . should try to catch criminals, but not at the expense of treating people with respect and dignity . . . To parents of African American youth . . . remember to school them about the police. They are not always their friends.

It's unfair that black parents have to teach this lesson while most white parents don't. But if we don't educate them early and often, we may be sending them to an early grave."

In this text, readers will learn strategies to deal with racial profiling in some of the "hotspots" where it is most likely to occur, including school, the street, cars, and court. They will learn about the unfairness of the prison-industrial complex that jails blacks more than whites for similar crimes and how to stay out of it. Readers will get "schooled," as Ava Greenwell says, in how to prepare emotionally if a police officer questions them. They will learn about their legal rights. They will also learn how traumatic racial profiling is, and how victims can heal themselves. Finally, they will learn ways that everyone—victims and allies—can join the fight for awareness of this epidemic of unfairness hiding in plain sight.

In February 2014, people of all races joined a protest against Florida's "stand your ground" law in the state's capital, Tallahassee. The law, which allows people to shoot anyone whom they feel threatened by, was widely blamed for the death of an innocent black youth, Trayvon Martin.

RACIAL PROFILING: A REAL PROBLEM

On September 22, 2013, two Hollywood actors, Cherie Johnson and Dennis White, stopped their car in South Carolina to take a picture of cotton fields—something Johnson had never seen before. When they got back to their car, they found a police car parked behind theirs with flashing lights. The officer pulled his gun, asked them harshly about whether or not they had drugs, and told Johnson they had a warrant for her arrest. After backing down and admitting that there was no such warrant, he searched the actors and their car and put them in handcuffs. When he found nothing, he finally let them go. He had no reason to suspect them of any wrongdoing, but he didn't offer an apology afterward.

Johnson and White were shattered and furious after their encounter with the police. White said he won't stop talking about the incident until "that racist cop" is reprimanded and punished. He said he had been racially profiled in the past. "We've been conditioned to just think that it's OK—that we have to just sweep it under the rug," White told the HLN

> Actor Cherie Johnson, shown here at the 11th Annual Palm Beach International Film Festival in Florida, is every inch a glamorous star. But that didn't stop her from being harassed by a police officer.

TV network. "But we're not doing that any more. We're fighting." The county where the officer works said it was "investigating" what had happened but hadn't come to any conclusions yet. Ironically, Johnson was the national cheer representative for First Lady Nancy Reagan's Just Say No to Drugs campaign in the 1980s.

In 2010, nineteen-year-old Luis Delgado was stopped by U.S. Border Patrol agents in southern Texas. He was born in Houston, but when he showed his U.S. birth certificate, immigration agents claimed his documents were fake because he had poor English skills. Despite his protests, the U.S. citizen was deported to Mexico. When the U.S. government finally allowed him to return three months later, he had lost his job.

On September 11, 2011, thirty-five-year-old Shoshanna Hebshi and two Indian American men were pulled off a plane in Detroit, Michigan. The Ohio resident, who is half-Jewish and half-Arab, was handcuffed, strip-searched, and jailed in a dirty cell by federal agents. After hours, during which she was not told why she was held, she was finally freed. "I was frightened and humiliated," Hebshi wrote on her blog, which later went viral. "As an American citizen and a mom, I'm really concerned about my children growing up in a country where your skin color and your name can put your freedom and liberty at risk at any time." The American Civil Liberties Union (ACLU) filed a lawsuit against several federal agencies on her behalf.

These are examples of racial profiling. Racial profiling is a form of official bullying by the government

Back in the 1970s, when the United States had a higher crime rate than it does today, the country had only three hundred thousand prisoners. In 2014, though, more than 2.3 million people were in U.S. jails and prisons. This explosive growth has led to the creation of a vast number of new jobs in law enforcement. Many prisons are private, for-profit facilities. This means that the people who own the companies that run them earn money from every convict who is in their prisons. Some call this the "prison-industrial complex." The increase in prisons has led to a major increase in the infrastructure of the judicial system. More people are hired to work in corrections departments, both as guards and in other roles.

The builders of these prisons make enough money to make big donations to lawmakers who vote on these issues, as the Corrections Documentary Project explains. The project's website notes "Correctional Corporations have amassed large political influence through government ties, lobbying power and campaign contributions, while attempting to convert the discourse of justice into the language of the marketplace." Because lawmakers need money to win elections, these contributions have the potential to affect whether a senator or congressperson would support building more prisons. According to a leading expert on crime policy, Michael H. Tonry, prison sentences here have become "vastly harsher than in any other country to which the United States would ordinarily be compared."

What makes this problem even worse is that although the United States has only 5 percent of the world's people, it has 25 percent of the world's prisoners—an astonishing 2.3 million people. The United States has the highest rate of imprisoned minorities in the world.

THE EXPLOSIVE GROWTH OF THE PRISON-INDUSTRIAL COMPLEX

that includes unreasonable detainment by police or other officers and goes on to unfair sentencing practices in courts. The U.S. Constitution guarantees rights for all of its citizens—but some people aren't being treated as equals because of their race or ethnicity.

Sadly, statistics show that if you are black, Hispanic, or of foreign descent, you have a higher chance of facing some form of racial profiling than white Americans. Muslims are especially likely to be subjected to racial profiling. Being traumatized in this way—with authority figures in complete control of your body, often pulling guns, handcuffing

Muslim protestors march past a police officer at a large antiwar rally in New York in 2011. They were protesting against the wars in Iraq and Afghanistan—and against Islamophobia (the fear and hatred of Muslims).

you, and touching you—can be very upsetting. And, unfortunately, there's no certain way of preventing it from happening again. However, you can find ways to strengthen yourself when it does happen.

If racial profiling has happened to you, you may wonder, "What should I have done?" If it has not happened to you, you may wonder, "How should I handle it?"

If it did happen to you and you didn't do everything perfectly, you may have a hard time forgiving yourself. But things can happen very fast, even if you're doing everything right. It is hard to know where to hold your ground and where to give in when you are dealing with grownups who literally have the power of your future—including your life and death—in their hands.

UNFAIR TREATMENT FOR BLACK MEN

According to statistics, black men are far more likely to be stopped by a police officer than white men. The ACLU analyzed federal data and found that although blacks and whites use marijuana at the same rate, blacks are almost four times as likely to be arrested for possessing it. Human Rights Watch said that between the years of 1980 and 2007, about one out of every three of the more than twenty-five million adults arrested for drugs was black. The organization's Jamie Fellner said, "Although whites and blacks use and sell drugs, the heavy hand of the law is more likely to fall on black shoulders." African American men are also ten times more likely to serve time in jail for possessing marijuana than white men.

Professor Michelle Alexander of Ohio State University started studying this issue and came to a reluctant realization. Although many Americans believe that we live in a "colorblind society," the U.S. criminal justice system is channeling young black men into prisons. She wrote about this problem in her book, *The New Jim Crow*. Jim Crow was a degrading nineteenth-century stereotype of a black man. For years after the Civil War, blacks in the South suffered from living under unfair "Jim Crow laws" that denied them rights such as drinking from the same water fountains as whites. Alexander came to believe that the incredibly high rate of imprisoning African Americans, especially for drug possession, is a systematic form of racism.

TIME TO MAKE WAR ON THE WAR ON DRUGS?

Alexander's groundbreaking book lays out the case that the main tool of this systematic racism has been the War on Drugs. This U.S. government campaign dates back to a declaration that President Richard Nixon made in 1970. The early laws that Congress passed and Nixon signed were aimed at rehabilitating, or curing, young people rather than imprisoning them. Since that time, however, attitudes have changed. In 1973, New York

State instituted the harsh Rockefeller drug laws. In the 1980s, the sudden death of a promising basketball player named Len Bias due to drugs inspired these mandatory minimum laws. These laws took away power from judges to consider outside factors in sentencing and made for harsher rulings.

According to Professor Alexander, these laws affect not just the 2.3 million people behind bars, but also 4.8 million others on probation or parole (mostly for nonviolent offenses). She is also concerned about prisoners who have completed their sentences. "This system depends on the prison label, not just prison time," she says. As she points out,

Demonstrators march in Washington, D.C., against the War on Drugs on June 17, 2013. Their concern was that the War on Drugs leads to the mass incarceration of young black men.

WHAT ARE OUR CONSTITUTIONAL RIGHTS?

The U.S. Constitution guarantees citizens a number of rights. Many legal experts believe that racial profiling violates parts of at least three of them:

The Fourth Amendment:

"The right of the people to be secure in their persons, houses, papers, and effects, against unreasonable searches and seizures, shall not be violated . . . but upon probable cause . . ."

This means that citizens should be free from searches unless the government (including the police) has reason to suspect them of a crime.

The Fifth Amendment:

"No person shall be compelled in any criminal case to be a witness against himself . . . without due process of law . . ."

This part of the amendment refers to suspects' rights to remain silent and not incriminate themselves.

The Fourteenth Amendment:

". . . nor shall any State . . . deny to any person within its jurisdiction the equal protection of the laws."

This refers to the idea that all American citizens deserve equal treatment under the law.

the punishment does not end after prisoners are released. Once a person answers a question such as, "Have you ever been convicted?" on a job application with a yes, it can be very difficult to get a job. Ex-convicts arc also denied a number of government services that poor people rely on, including public housing, educational opportunities, and more. They can be automatically denied the chance to serve on juries. In eleven states, people who have served prison sentences are denied the right to vote for the rest of their lives. This disproportionately affects black voting patterns and could even change the results of elections.

The fact that one out of three black men can expect to be arrested in their lifetimes destabilizes the entire black community by destroying families, opportunities, and neighborhoods. A black child today is less likely to be raised by both parents than a black child who was born during slavery. The main reason for this is that so many African American men are in jail. As Alexander points out, many more African Americans are in prison, in jail, on parole, or on probation than there were slaves in 1850, ten years before the Civil War started.

EVERYBODY LOSES

Racial profiling can cause problems for police officers, too. The police can't do their jobs alone. They need citizens to be their eyes and ears when a crime is taking place. They need people to call in for help, and they need witnesses for trials. But people who distrust the police refuse to help them. When people can't feel safe,

when they don't feel as if they will be treated fairly because of their skin color, they are less likely to come forward and speak to the police if they see something dangerous. That makes it harder to make neighborhoods safe.

Another problem is that some people who are addicted to drugs do want to get help. However, if they are only going to be put in jail instead of getting help, they will not be motivated to stop. That means the person's drug problem will not get solved.

A third problem is that it erodes the rights of all people. The strict laws that jail minorities in order to (allegedly) increase safety mean that everyone has to give up some of the

Virginia started a community policing unit to ease the tensions between the police and residents. Here, Officer Juan Damian visits store owner Dora Escobar in Langley In July 2009.

civil rights guaranteed in the U.S. Constitution to protect their "safety." The police have become much more aggressive, and the government is taking more liberties with people's private information. Not only that, but the United States' incredibly high overall incarceration rate means that the numbers of white people put in prison is also far higher than it is in other countries.

But perhaps the biggest problem with racial profiling is that it is wrong. People in many other countries are shocked and appalled at the United States' high incarceration rate and its racial profiling. We live in an era in which prejudice has been decreasing, and most Americans believe in justice and fairness for everyone. This makes it ironic that this serious problem is taking place right under our noses and that relatively few people are aware of just how serious it is.

OTHER AMERICANS UNDER SCRUTINY

Most of the Hispanic Americans who live in the United States are citizens. But as many as twelve million undocumented workers have crossed into the United States, mostly from Mexico, to do low-paying jobs such as harvesting crops. This has become a problem for the Hispanics who are here legally. For example, Arizona passed a controversial immigration law called SB 1070 that requires authorities to check the ID of anyone they suspect is in the country illegally.

Supporters say the law is fair because people of any race could be asked to show their IDs. However, people are not generally required to carry any kind of identifying papers with them in other parts of the United States unless they are operating a vehicle or doing some other kind of activity that needs ID. Opponents say that this law puts all Hispanics under constant scrutiny, since Hispanic heritage is the most common reason that people in the Southwest are suspected of being there illegally.

Muslims have also faced a number of problems as well. Some have been required to "register" under a special program. The FBI has admitted to spying on Muslim neighborhoods, including mosques, and imprisoning up to a thousand Muslim men who were later released as innocent with no charges after being held for long periods. Muslims also face frequent harassment at airports, which can cause them to miss their flights.

Police and federal agents are the gatekeepers for the criminal justice system. In his book *Arrest-Proof Yourself: An Ex-Cop Reveals How Easy It Is for Anyone to Get Arrested, How Even a Single Arrest Could Ruin Your Life, and What to Do If the Police Get in Your Face*, author Dale Carson says the best way to minimize the impact of racial profiling is to avoid the police's attention as much as possible. How?

First, obey the laws. Don't carry pot. Don't shoplift. Don't deface property. Don't hang around with people who do criminal activities. It's wrong. And chances are, you'll get caught.

Second, stay away from places where the police are likely to be cruising around. If you live in an especially high-crime neighborhood, stay off the streets as much as possible. Police are especially on the lookout for criminal activity that takes place after midnight. You need to do your homework and get a good night's rest anyway. So stay off the streets at night.

Third, appearances matter. If you dress in certain ways that identify you as a gang member, or in a manner similar to criminals,

BEFORE YOU GO OUT: GET YOUR WALLET READY

There are several important things you should keep in your wallet at all times. If you have one, you should carry your driver's license. Also, carry a lawyer's name and phone number with you, if you have one. Another extremely helpful document is the ALCU's Bust Card. It is a foldable, wallet-sized guide to your rights and responsibilities in case you are stopped by the police, immigration agents, or the FBI. You can find a Bust Card online at http://www.aclu.org/files/assets/bustcard_eng_20100630.pdf and print it out free of charge.

the police aren't going to know you're actually an A+ student. They're going to suspect you and keep an eye on you. Dressing more conservatively may help you avoid trouble.

Fourth, if police are at a crime scene, stay away. Don't stay and gawk. Criminals often like to return to the scene of the crime. Sometimes police question those who are in the crowds. They also take pictures of the crowd. You don't want to be in those pictures. Carson also notes that

CRIME SCENE DO

if a police cruiser drives by, the police are looking for unusual behavior. So "whatever you're doing, just keep doing it," he says. If you're looking at the sky, leaning against a lamppost, keep leaning. Girls, don't start looking in your bags. Boys, don't suddenly reach into your jacket. If you're walking, keep walking. If you're jogging, stay at the same pace. But don't start running. Remember, the police are supposed to protect innocent people. They are SUPPOSED to look for suspicious behavior. When they question someone, it may not just be racial profiling. However, as little contact with the police is desirable.

If you really want to prepare yourself in case

If you see police at a crime scene, stay away. The police may think your curiosity is more than casual and could start asking you questions.

you are racially profiled, another thing you can do is to learn as much as you can about the legal system. There are a number of library books and websites that you can consult. One organization that can help you is the American Civil Liberties Union (http://www. ACLU.org). The legal book publisher Nolo (http:// www.nolo.com) has an extensive free legal advice section on its website. Nolo also has a national database of lawyers. It can be helpful to have the name and number of a criminal defense attorney just in case of trouble. You or your parents or guardians can use a site such as Nolo or ask for recommendations from people you know. You or your parents may want to talk to the lawyer briefly to see if he or she would be a good fit for you. Lawyers will often give brief consultations free of charge. Carry the lawyer's name and phone number with you.

IF YOU ARE STOPPED ON THE STREET

If you are worried about being racially profiled, there are steps you can take. One is to know about how to handle police. Learning how to stay calm, respectful, and in control of your words, body language, and emotions is something you should practice with helpful adults or your peers.

If an officer calls you over or comes up to you, don't run away. If he or she starts to ask you questions, you can ask, "Am I in some kind of trouble, officer?" That will let you know if you are under suspicion and if the officer intends to detain you. Police can ask you questions—as anybody can—but according to the New York Civil Liberties Union (NYCLU), "Police may stop and briefly detain you only if there is reasonable suspicion that you committed, are committing or are about to commit a crime."

If the answer is no, ask, "Officer, am I free to go?" If the officer says yes, then leave. Say as little as possible. Anything you say to a police officer can be used against you in court in ways you can't imagine. If you don't want to talk and the officer says you are not free to go, you can say, "I would like to remain silent."

In most states, you are not required to carry ID and you don't have to show ID to a police officer. But it's a good idea to carry it. The NYCLU says, "If you are issued a summons or arrested, however, and you refuse to produce ID or tell officers who you are, the police may detain you until you can be positively identified."

If an officer asks if he or she can look in your bag or backpack, politely say no. You can say something like, "My mother/teacher/pastor advised me to say no to searches." If they do it anyway, say, "I do not consent to this search." They may search your bag anyway. Don't try to stop them. But if you end up in court, your refusal to give consent could help you. There are exceptions to this rule. Government agents have the right to inspect your luggage if you're going on a plane, for instance.

Police officers and security guards in certain other places, such as museums, subways, and courthouses, have the right to inspect your bags, too.

The law requires that officers have "probable cause" to frisk you. Probable cause means that the police have reasonable grounds for suspecting you of committing a crime. If an officer insists on frisking you, don't resist, touch the officer, or make any trouble. You can and should say, "I do not consent to this search." However, any physical resistance could get you arrested.

IN YOUR CAR

One of the most common places people can

Young black men often face situations such as these, whether or not they are justified.

be profiled is in a car. A Department of Justice report found that blacks and Hispanics were three times more likely to be searched than white drivers during a during a traffic stop.

According to the National Motorists Association, a young African man named Nelson Walker was pulled over by state troopers in Maryland. The police claimed he wasn't wearing a seatbelt. The officers searched his car for drugs, but they didn't find any. Instead of letting him go, they started taking apart his car, removing the seat panel, door panel, and part of the sunroof. The officers again found nothing. They left with no

Knowing your rights—as well as your responsibilities—if you ge a ticket is something that every teen, especially black teen should know before getting on the road.

apologies—only giving Walker a screwdriver to repair his car. The ACLU filed suit on his behalf.

Also named in that lawsuit were an elderly black couple named Charles and Etta Carter. Although they had no justification for probable cause, Maryland state troopers searched their car with drug-sniffing dogs. When the dogs didn't find anything, the Carters' belongings were thrown along the highway. There, their possessions, including their daughter's wedding dress, were urinated on and trampled on by the police dogs.

While most drivers don't face that kind of abuse, Dr. Jawanza Kunjufu, an education expert and author of *Raising Black Boys*, advises teens—particularly teens of color—to be prepared before they get into a car. The first step, he says, is to make sure that the police don't have any excuse to make trouble for you. Have a valid license and keep it with you. Put your wallet on the dashboard or some easy-to-reach place. Don't drive if you don't have insurance. If you've been out with your friends, check the car thoroughly to make sure that they haven't left any illegal substances in your car. Make sure that the car is working properly and that it does not have problems such as broken headlights, which can result in a pullover. Don't drink or take drugs in a car. And don't let any of your friends do it, either. Make sure they aren't carrying any illegal substances. Follow the laws when you drive. Don't drive too slowly or too quickly. Don't text and drive. Driving is serious business. Police are on the lookout for erratic behavior by drivers—as they should be.

IF POLICE STOP YOU

If the police pull you over, stay in the car and wait for an officer to approach you. Be polite. If an officer asks for ID, show him or her your driver's license, registration, and proof of insurance. The officer may ask to search your car. In certain cases, your car can be searched without a warrant. To protect yourself later, you should state that you do not consent to a search. However, the police officer may insist anyway. If so, don't stand in the officer's way. Instead, stay very calm and remember every detail you can about the incident for later.

If you're suspected of drunk driving (driving while intoxicated, or DWI), you will be asked to take a breath-alcohol and coordination test. If you fail the tests, or if you refuse to take them, you will be arrested, your driver's license may be suspended, and your car may be taken away. If you are arrested, your car will be subject to a search.

The police may frisk you. You can still object to being frisked. Again, you can ask if you are free to go. If the police ask to search your car or backpack, tell them you do not consent to a search. They may search anyway. Don't get in their way.

If you get a ticket for an offense such as speeding, the police may take your driver's license away to ensure that

you will pay the ticket. To avoid this kind of aggravation, you can get a bond card. The police will take the bond card instead of your license. You can get a bond card through your insurance or through the Automobile Association of America (AAA). Not all police departments will take a bond card, but most do. Of course, don't forget to pay the fine!

WHAT IF YOU FEEL YOU HAVE BEEN UNFAIRLY TREATED?

During the incident, attempt to memorize the officer's name and badge number. Remember as many details as you can. As soon as possible, write down everything you remember.

When police start inspecting a car, it can be hard to know how to act. Remember to keep a clear head and pay attention to what they do.

Note what the officer said, his or her demeanor, what you said, if you consented to a search or not, exactly where you were stopped, and what reason the officer gave. If the officer complained that you had a broken taillight but that wasn't true, try to take a photo with a time stamp as soon as possible after the incident.

If you are given a ticket you feel is unfair, figure out the court date and go. Gather all the evidence you can, and ask for police evidence. Insist on seeing the tape of the incident as well as the full report.

CHAPTER 3

It's hard to believe, but, even in the old days, students weren't always perfect. Recently, the Advancement Project, a national civil rights group that works to cut down school arrests, made a public service ad that was both funny and sad. It showed scenes from old TV shows of kids doing things they weren't supposed to—talking on their cell phones in class, skipping school, getting into a fight. What did the teachers do? In the fight example, the teacher made two girls shake hands.

ZERO TOLERANCE

Today, schools have gotten much tougher. On April 20, 1999, two white boys opened fire and killed thirteen people at Columbine High School in Colorado. After that, many schools got metal detectors, drug-sniffing dogs, mandatory drug testing, and police officers in schools. They also started harsh "zero tolerance" policies, which made tough punishments for even minor offenses. That meant incidents that would have provoked a stern lecture from a teacher in the past could now lead to expulsion, suspension, or even an arrest.

Students in poorer neighborhoods are more likely to go to schools with harsh policies.

More and more students feel they are being treated like criminals by facing such precautions as metal detectors and police inspections when they go to school.

Since more minority students attend these schools, they are also more likely to be expelled for extremely minor infractions, such as not wearing the right clothes (uniform violations), speaking too loudly, or even rolling their eyes. During the 2011–2012 school year, 675 Maryland kindergarten students got out-of-school suspensions for such small offenses as being disrespectful to the teacher or using bad language, according to the NAACP Legal Defense Fund.

Eleventh-grader Diane Tran of Willis, Texas, spent twenty-four hours in jail for missing class. The straight-A student held down two jobs to help support her siblings. After Houston's KHOU-TV station reported her story, Texas was criticized for turning good students into criminals.

Twelve-year-old Nalani Bolden was suspended from school because she broke several small rules—she was late to class, she talked too much, and used her cell phone. But she didn't get the telephone message about her suspension. So when she came to school to take her midterm exams, she was arrested for trespassing. A deputy handcuffed her, led her through a gathering of students, and put her in a police car.

MAKING SCHOOL POSITIVE: STAYING OUT OF THE PIPELINE

Getting your high school degree is one of the best ways to secure a better future for yourself. Whatever you do, get your high school diploma. Hill Harper says in his book *Letters to a Young Brother*, "What you don't realize is that school does not control you . . . you control school . . . Schools stay open because of your attendance . . . By controlling school I mean getting your needs met . . . sometimes it's your job to help the teachers help you. The great Muhammad Ali said, 'I try to learn as much as I can because I know nothing compared to what I need to know.' Be smart, know what you don't know, and do not be afraid to learn it."

As unpleasant as they may be, many of the strict rules in schools can help you gain skills that will make you better at navigating the adult world effectively. You can gain valuable discipline that will increase your chances of success in the business world. Whatever you do, remember that the primary purpose of school is getting your degree.

Use standard English with adults, such as teachers and principals. Be sure to express yourself respectfully even if you disagree with them. Learning to use these skills is an incredibly valuable life tool.

Follow the rules. If there is a dress code, don't break it. If you aren't allowed to bring cell phones, don't bring one. Don't get out of your seat or leave a classroom without permission. Be on time.

Get a reputation for being reliable, responsible, and a good student. If you are having trouble with a subject, ask for extra help from the teacher and pay attention. If you still have trouble, watch an

School can be a lot more pleasant if you follow the rules. Some of them can actually provide useful life skills.

educational YouTube video or ask any of your friends if they want to start an after-school study group. Get teachers on your side. Treat them like human beings. If you have a teacher who truly dislikes you, enlist the help of another adult. You may need a parent-teacher conference. Get after-school help if you're falling behind. Learn everything you can—you never know when you're going to need it. Do your home-work. Pay attention in class. In social studies class, pay extra attention to learning about how the gov-ernment works. Take special care to learn about the Constitution and the Bill of Rights. Knowing your legal rights is always helpful.

THE (POLICE) STATE OF FLORIDA

Florida arrests more students than any other state. Wansley Walters, the secretary of the Florida Department of Juvenile Justice, told the *Orlando Sentinel*, "The vast majority of children being arrested in schools are not committing criminal acts." In 2012, 67 percent of the arrests of students in Florida schools were for misdemeanors. These included disorderly conduct, which can include anything from not wearing a school uniform to refusing to take a cell phone out of a pocket to being too loud in class. Less than 5 per-cent of the children arrested in Florida that year faced weapons charges.

Avoid fights in school. Fights are a leading cause of suspensions. If you have a disagreement, argue your side with calm words, not fists or a raised voice. Don't use racially or sexually insulting language with anyone. Those words can be used against you later. Never use your computer to express hateful thoughts toward anyone.

If some rules seem truly unreasonable, join an organization or create a petition to try to get them changed. Don't take it on yourself to break them—you'll just get in trouble. Besides, when you go to work, you'll probably have to deal with rules that you don't like, too. It's just part of life.

IF YOU DO GET IN TROUBLE, KNOW YOUR RIGHTS

School officials have the right to search a student without a warrant if they believe the student has drugs, weapons, or other illegal substances. School officials can pat down students. They can ask students to empty their pockets, backpacks, and lockers. If they find something illegal, they can call the police.

Students should know that their lockers, backpacks, and wallets are not legally considered private in school.

However, if you have done nothing wrong and there is no evidence against you, you are not obliged to talk to the school officials. If you are going to talk, insist on getting a parent or other responsible adult to help you. If you and your guardians are not satisfied with the results of a punishment and feel it is unjust, take it to a higher level. If you reach the highest level, then attend a school board meeting and protest. If that doesn't work, you might consider taking your story to a local newspaper.

1. What can one person do to stop racial profiling?

2. What steps do I need to go through to start a group to fight racial profiling?

3. What are some Internet resources or online groups that I can use to learn about racial profiling?

4. What are some of the greatest needs of families who have been affected by racial profiling, and are there ways for young people to help them?

5. If I want to educate myself more about the subject of racial profiling, what resources do you recommend?

6. What arguments can I use to get others interested in the cause of racial profiling?

7. If I've been profiled, do I have a responsibility to share my experience even if it brings up painful memories?

8. If people are profiled more than once, do they usually feel as scared the second or third time as they do the first?

9. How can I help a friend who has been racially profiled?

10. What can I or my club do to help stop the school-to-prison pipeline?

10 GREAT QUESTIONS TO ASK A CIVIL RIGHTS ACTIVIST

If the police detain you, take the situation very seriously. The police have a number of options if they find a minor, or young person, behaving in a manner they find questionable. They may issue a warning and release the minor. Sometimes they can hold the minor until a parent comes to pick him or her up. But sometimes, they may put the minor in custody and refer the case to juvenile court.

WHAT HAPPENS AFTER AN ARREST?

If you are arrested—whether or not racial profiling was involved—the police may handcuff you. They may put you in a police car and take you to a police station. They may require proof of your identity. Give them ID, but don't tell them anything but your name and address. Say that you want your parents with you. After a reasonable time, you should be allowed to call your parents. The call may be recorded, so give few details. Practice keeping your mouth shut. Do not try to talk your way out of the situation. If you have a lawyer, call him or her. If you can't afford one, ask for a court-appointed lawyer. You should not sign any statements until you've spoken with a lawyer. Police officers

Any minor who is taken into custody should insist on having parents or guardians with him or her before telling police any details about the case.

are supposed to read people who they are questioning their Miranda rights, but sometimes they wait a very long time and pretend you aren't a suspect when you are.

If you are taken into police custody, there may be a prosecutor who can dismiss the case, handle it informally, or file formal charges. Some factors the prosecutor may consider are: the age of a minor; the severity of the crime that he or she is being charged with; if there is any evidence against the minor; and if the family seems to have much influence over the minor's behavior.

If the case is handled informally, no formal charge will be filed against the student. However, he or she will probably appear before a judge and may face certain consequences, such as paying a fine, getting counseling, performing community service, or getting probation.

If the student gets probation, he or she will be required to have meetings

Joan Cox is a probation officer who monitors kids in the juvenile justice system at Northwestern High School in Hyattsville, Maryland. Students on probation must sign in and out with her during school.

with a law officer, called a probation officer, for a certain period of time, such as six months or a year. The meetings can involve drug testing. The probation officer will decide when they take place. When a probation officer sets a meeting time, it is extremely important to show up at the correct time. At the meetings, try to show ways that you are making good-faith efforts to improve your life, such as getting a job or going to self-help meetings. Missing meetings can result in harsh consequences, such as being sent to formal court.

A young person may be charged or "arraigned" in front of a juvenile court. In juvenile court, the judge will make a ruling based on the seriousness of the offense and the young person's efforts at self-improvement. Some of the judge's options include requiring counseling, reimbursing a victim, obeying curfews, or even placing the student in a juvenile detention home. If the offense is serious enough, the

MIRANDA RIGHTS

Miranda rights are a warning in the United States that police are supposed to give to criminal suspects before they are questioned. It includes words such as telling the suspected person that he or she has "the right to remain silent, the right to legal counsel, and the right to be told that anything he/she says can be used in court against" him or her. The Miranda rule is based on the Fifth Amendment to the U.S. Constitution and the right for citizens not to incriminate themselves.

student may be charged as an adult, which can result in more serious sentencing.

GOING TO COURT

If at all possible, get a criminal defense lawyer. If your family cannot afford a lawyer, ask about court-appointed lawyers. Be aware that many court-appointed lawyers have large caseloads and cope with this by making deals. If you are innocent, think carefully before agreeing to one. Be aware that you have rights. Sometimes there are reasons to put off a court date. One of the most important is that you will want to have a copy of the police report and any evidence that the police have against you.

Any criminal charge should be taken very seriously. Gathering witnesses, getting good legal advice, and acting with dignity and maturity in the courtroom are all ways of improving your chances for the best possible outcome.

Remember, a lot of police cruisers now have cameras. You will want the full report and the tape before trial. You will also want to gather all the evidence you can about your innocence. For instance, if there is anyone who could be a witness in your defense, tell your lawyer about that person.

When you go to court, dress formally and respectfully. Court is a serious and intimidating place. Act with your best manners. If you are willing to make a deal, show remorse and say why you would not repeat the action. Find out if you can pay a fine or do community service, rather than serving jail time.

Judges do have some leeway, so be sure to present your most positive side. Think of any contributions you make to the community or any mitigating factors that

Don't Lose Your Paperwork

Some traffic offenses or other offenses may require you to go to court on a certain day. Read any ticket or any letters you get from the court system carefully. Hold onto them. Put the dates on your calendar and do not miss them. If there is a fine that needs to be paid by a certain day, make sure that you pay it, unless you decide to take it to court. If you are expected in court for other reasons, do not miss the date or you can get into serious trouble. This is one place where organization and timeliness count!

contributed to your present trouble. If you get community service or probation, make sure you never miss an appointment or a commitment. Minor infractions often mean that kids get in more serious trouble.

EXPUNGING A RECORD

If you are convicted of a crime, it might be sealed if you are a minor. That means you will not need to answer yes to the question "Have you ever been convicted?" after you have served your sentence. If your conviction is not sealed, you might still be able to get it expunged, or removed, from your record after you are eighteen. Although you may have to go to court and pay a fine to get your conviction removed, it could be one of the best investments you ever make.

MYTHS AND FACTS

MYTH

Police only stop a person because they have evidence that he or she may have committed a crime.

FACT

Police are allowed to detain people briefly if they have probable cause that these people have committed or are about to commit a crime.

MYTH

Most of the people behind bars in the United States are dangerous criminals.

FACT

Most of the prisoners in the United States are there for relatively minor, nonviolent offenses, especially drug-related offenses.

MYTH

More black Americans than white Americans take drugs, so it's natural that the arrest, conviction, and jail-time rates would be more severe for African Americans.

FACT

Blacks and whites take drugs at approximately the same rate, so the penalties given to blacks are not based on fairness.

Being racially profiled can be a shattering experience. It can make victims feel terrified, humiliated, and deeply discouraged about their future. If racial profiling happens to you, you may have a traumatic reaction to it. After Nalani Bolden was arrested for returning to school to take an exam, she couldn't face going back to school. She had trouble eating and sleeping. "It was horrible," Nalani told the *Orlando Sentinel*. "I don't want to go back to public school. I'm afraid it will happen again."

A PAINFUL EXPERIENCE

People who have been racially profiled can feel many of the following symptoms:

Physical symptoms: Dizziness, sweaty palms, racing heart, crying, stomach problems, pain that is unexplained, mood swings
Behavioral symptoms: Fear of going out or being alone, lack of hunger or eating too much, sleeplessness
Emotional symptoms: Shame, anger, fear, loss of purpose, flashbacks, sensory memories
Attitude changes: Sabotaging your own success, bitterness, helplessness, rage, feeling danger in safe places

One of the problems with racial profiling is that it is unlike many other problems, such as bulimia, which can be changed by attitude. No one is immune from having it happen again because it comes from the outside. However, there are things that can help. First, there are therapists who specialize in treating post-traumatic stress disorder (PTSD). Even if you don't have access to therapists, there may be wise adults in your life you can reach out to for help. They could include a pastor, priest, rabbi, or imam. A school counselor, a teacher, or a counselor at a low-cost clinic might also be able to help. There are many books on the subject of trauma that can give helpful ideas about how to overcome it. And, of course, talking to friends can lessen your suffering.

Positive Steps You Can Take

One bright note is that there are good cures for stress. Exercise is one of them. Meditation is another. Ways in which you can take charge of your own life, like learning a new skill (cooking is something you can always use), will put you ahead of the game.

Anger can be a righteous emotion that can encourage you to fight for social justice. You have every right to fight for your own rights, and you should. Fighting

Being racially profiled can lead to depression and anger. But there are techniques you can use to overcome it.

for yourself is a way of making society more just. It also might make you remember to seek justice for others. The best revenge is to become the best individual you can be.

Remember that no matter how someone tries to label you, you are a unique individual. That uniqueness is a precious gift. Try to find ways to express yourself creatively. When bad feelings come up, name them. Keep a journal so that you become aware of things that trigger bad feelings. You may need to describe your experience and your memories many times before you can release them. Be forgiving of yourself—many people feel ashamed that they didn't do more to protect themselves in a situation where they were traumatized. Don't forget that when people are scared, they are not always in control of their emotions.

Remember that your sufferings are shared by many people who have been through similar experiences. Have hope that they found ways to cope, and you will, too.

Reach out to your friends and family—especially people who have a lot of positive energy. It can be natural to hide away when you've been put through an experience with others. But chances are that your friends will be feeling empathy and kindness toward you. Let them give

Meditation and listening to music are good ways of recovering a sense of wholeness when you are feeling as if you've lost your sense of self through racial profiling.

you the same kind of support you would no doubt give them if the situation were reversed.

Prepare yourself in case it happens again. Make sure that you use as many practical tips as you can, but also make sure you strengthen yourself emotionally. Many of the world's greatest leaders, thinkers, and creators went through unfair and humiliating experiences in their lives but didn't give up. Don't you give up, either.

Take pride in your history. Remember the humiliations of people in past generations. They overcame experiences much worse than racial profiling. Dr. Jawanza Kunjufu recommends *The Souls of Black Folk* by W. E. B. Du Bois. But that is just one of many books by and about people of different ethnicities who helped to make our country great.

Don't forget to take care of yourself physically. That means getting out into the sun for at least thirty minutes a day if it's warm enough. Also, try to exercise as much as possible. It will not only help you get your frustrations out, but it will also get chemicals called endorphins flowing through your body. Endorphins help people feel more positive.

Look for a sense of long-term purpose in your life. Think of important goals, such as getting a degree, going to college, or taking on the job of your dreams.

W. E. B. Dubois (1868–1963) was one of America's greatest black scholars, writers, and civil rights activists.

HOW TO MAKE A SAFETY CHECKLIST

If you find that you are feeling more and more negative and think that you could be in danger of harming yourself, you should make a safety checklist with someone you trust. Consider making the list a contract that you sign in front of the other person. In it, you should spell out how much of a danger you feel you might be to yourself or others. Carry your safety checklist with you at all times.

Include the names and phone numbers of people you can talk to on the list. This should include your doctor and/or therapist. Be sure to list at least one suicide prevention hotline. One example is the National Hopeline Network at 1-800-SUICIDE.

List what you can do to change your outlook when you feel that you are becoming a danger to yourself. These may include exercising, having a special treat just for that occasion, reading something positive, or even just watching a silly movie.

If you do sign the safety checklist as a contract, pick someone important to you to witness it. Signing it in front of a witness you care about won't guarantee that you won't harm yourself, but it could hold you back. Remember, a life that's lost is gone forever.

Consider using your personal experience to help others in some way. That could mean tutoring younger kids or taking direct action, as in the next chapter. Do something small every day to reach toward that goal.

WHAT NOT TO DO WHEN YOU'RE HURTING

You already have enough problems on your plate because you're a teenager. Teenage brains are more primed to be emotional and extreme than adult brains. That means emotional slights and attacks can potentially hurt more and make you feel angrier and more stressed than an adult.

Some things to avoid doing when you are feeling upset are using drugs or alcohol, oversleeping, and avoiding other people. One problem some people have is rumination—thinking the same negative thoughts over and over. If you find yourself ruminating, get up and change your activity. Also, actively fight your thoughts. Reframe the message your brain is giving you. Instead of saying, "I'll never be safe," say, "I'll always be strong, no matter what I face," for instance.

FIND YOUR OWN RESILIENCY

Experiences like racial profiling can be deeply traumatizing, but many young people have a built-in quality that helps them get through tough times. That quality is resilience. There are many ways that people exhibit that quality. It can be as simple as finding something beautiful or funny on your toughest days. It can involve trying weight lifting in the school gym for the

Learning to reframe thoughts so that they are more positive and make you feel encouraged to engage with other people is an important skill for anyone to master.

first time, or writing a list of things you feel grateful for. It's finding ways to bounce back from life's tough blows. In author Ellis Cose's *The End of Anger: A New Generation's Take on Race and Rage*, he writes, "'It's become clear there's this thing called resiliency, where if it doesn't kill you it makes you stronger, and black people have that,' observed Carl Bell, the psychiatrist from Chicago, who has speculated on why the black suicide rate was less than half that of whites. The Reverend Jesse Jackson told me much the same thing. 'Our strength is measured by absorbing trauma without being embittered. Those who cannot survive trauma commit suicide or they use liquor and drugs to drown the sensation of pain.'"

CHAPTER 6

HOW TEENS CAN MAKE A DIFFERENCE

One of the most positive things about today's young people is that they may be the least racist generation in America's history, thanks to the gains of the civil rights movement. Students of all races and ethnicities generally believe in equality. Many young people have friends of different races. Because racial profiling is an issue that affects them or their friends so directly, young people of all races have a motivation and an important stake in the fight against it. Many would be likely to take positive steps

This generation of young people may be the most racially and socially integrated in America's history.

to help end racial profiling if they knew what was happening to their black, Hispanic, Muslim, Indian, and other friends who face this form of harassment. What can young people do, individually and together, to help end it?

INFORM AND WITNESS

If you have seen or experienced racial profiling, you can find opportunities to share what you know. Talking about being racially profiled can help others understand how serious the problem really is. All the feelings that it brings up—from anger to helplessness or shame—can be used to empower positive action. Publicizing any real-life examples or statistics you've discovered while doing research can also help others understand the scope of the problem.

According to a study by researchers at the University of Chicago, large numbers of young people of all races and ethnicities are using social media platforms such as Twitter and Facebook for "participatory politics." This includes acts such as starting a political group online, circulating a blog about a political issue, or forwarding political videos to friends. Today's tech-savvy kids are finding new ways to use technology to change the world. Whether it's posting anti–racial profiling events on Facebook, making a YouTube video, or live-tweeting a racial profiling that they're witnessing, the members of this generation are one step—if not more—ahead of adults.

If you are concerned that you might be treated unfairly, you could make a recording of the event. Is that legal? In many places, it is. However, you should check your state's laws.

If you have a record function on your cell phone, you can discreetly turn it on. The New York Civil Liberties Union developed a free smartphone application (it works with both iPhones and Androids) to let New Yorkers monitor illegal stop-and-frisk confrontations and other police misbehavior. It is called the Stop and Frisk Watch app and can be found at http://www.nyclu.org/app. The app allows bystanders to fully document encounters with the police and alert community members when a street stop is in progress.

If the police give you grief for recording them, the law can help you fight back. Hadiyah Charles, from Brooklyn, New York, was shoved, handcuffed, arrested, and held in jail for ninety minutes for using her smartphone to record police officers. The officers were harshly questioning and frisking three black youth who had been fixing a bike down the street. The New York Civil Liberties Union filed a suit on her behalf.

CAN YOU RECORD THE POLICE?

A University of Chicago study found that virtually all teens have access to the Internet and get news from it. Smartphones and iPods are giving today's teens even more power. For instance, a seventeen-year-old New Yorker

named Alvin secretly recorded a very uncomfortable meeting with police who appeared to be harassing him in 2011.

START AN ANTI-RACISM CLUB

In your school, there are a number of ways that you can raise awareness about the issue of racial profiling. There is power in numbers, so find group support. Start an antiracism club. To do so, you may need to find out how clubs are formed in your school, and then you can find a teacher who will sponsor the club. Ask if there is a budget for clubs and if you are entitled to school funding. When you gather a small group, pick a name and

Young people today have better technological tools for fighting racism than any generation in the past.

design a logo. You may want to find ways to get members—such as having a flash mob in the cafeteria (get permission first), putting on a skit, putting up flyers, or setting up a recruitment table.

A recruitment table is a great way to draw interest to your club. Make a paper or cloth banner that you can put in front of the table with the club's name and logo. Decorate trifold boards with informative text, photos, and infographics for the table itself, or create posters to put up on a wall behind you. You can create handouts about the club, listing its meeting times and mission. A racial profiling fact sheet, using statistics drawn from this book or other sources,

One way an antiracism group can grow is out of natural conversations students have when they are just hanging out together during school breaks, at lunch, or after school.

would make another good handout. You could also consider handing out copies of the ACLU's Bust Card. Have a sign-up sheet, and ask for people's numbers and e-mail addresses. And, unless it goes against school policy, it never hurts to give out treats like candy!

Make a website or Facebook page for your club and remember to add new information to it on a regular basis. In fact, you can assign a different club member to update it each day. The members can post about news or events, ask provocative questions, and share their own experiences.

Once your club is up and running, it might inspire other clubs if you can get recognition for your efforts. The first step is to document, document, document. Write down what you've done. Take pictures. Make videos. Send out the news to everyone you can think of via press releases, social media, and more.

TAKE A CLOSE LOOK AT YOUR OWN SCHOOL

One club goal could be to take some time to talk openly and nonjudgmentally about race. Learning to talk honestly about race—creating a space where people of good will can ask honest questions—can be healing, even when it's hard. Not talking about it can be toxic. Today, many people say they're "colorblind." But, according to writer Errol Lewis, that doesn't make sense. Everyone notices and judges other people by their appearance. Lewis says, "It's not that people aren't trying. The problem is that Americans, wishing to bring about a colorblind society,

If you believe that racial profiling is a problem at your school, start building up a case to prove it. See if you can find statistics on whether the school has a higher rate of suspending ethnic minorities. Try to figure out if people of different backgrounds are punished the same way if they break the same school rules. Collect anecdotes. If you or your friends know anyone who has been suspended or punished for minor infractions, talk to that person. You can band together and provide a strong case. Go to school board meetings and speak up.

You might also want to do a project about your school or schools in your area to find out how many students have been suspended, expelled, and arrested. Look into what punishments kids at different schools received for the same misbehavior. If the punishments seem overly harsh, or if race seems to be a factor in how kids are punished, you can use that information to create a report for the school board.

often end up being colormute—fearful of offending, we simply clam up about race and racism, confining our blunt, not-politically-correct sentiments or questions to small groups of trusted friends and family."

Once you've opened up to each other, you might want to promote a school-wide activity, such as Teaching Tolerance's Mix It Up Day. Mix It Up Day encourages kids to sit at tables with kids of other races and get to know them.

EDUCATE YOURSELF

It always helps to learn more about the scope of a problem. Michelle Alexander's *The New Jim Crow* is an excellent place to start learning about racial profiling. But many of the websites and other volumes mentioned in the back section of this book can help as well.

Try enlisting a teacher's help. A number of organizations have curriculum guides for teachers to help promote awareness of racial profiling and other justice issues. Check out some of these activities and lessons. Share some of the ones you like with your

Teachers can be a tremendous help, both by mentoring teens and by standing behind students who are trying to start groups to increase awareness of important social issues, such as racial profiling.

favorite social studies teacher. The teacher might decide to do them in class. Some of the lessons could also work out of class as well. They could be done in workshops, club meetings, or assemblies.

The Teaching Tolerance website (http://www.tolerance .org) is run by the Southern Poverty Law Center. It has a wealth of ideas, activities, and information that students, teachers, and clubs can use to promote racial fairness. The Not in Our Schools section of the organization

Protests can be a useful way of getting a message out. These people protested at Barney's, a department store in New York, after several black shoppers said they were racially profiled there in October 2013.

Not in Our Town's website (http://www.niot.org/nios) has dozens of age-appropriate activities and sources of information.

The National Education Association (NEA) has started its own Campaign to End Racial Profiling. The campaign's website is a rich source of tips, lessons, and resources. It includes a one-page handout to inform students about racial profiling that any group or individual can use. It also has a "Know Your Rights Postcard" that reminds young people of their rights. The NEA worked with a number of anti-hate organizations to develop the curriculum, which involves many different ways of actively addressing racism.

LETTING THE GOVERNMENT HEAR YOUR OUTRAGE

Another way to combat racial profiling is to push lawmakers to pass laws outlawing it. One way to let government leaders know that you are against racial profiling is to take part in marches or other protests opposing it. You could even think about helping organize this kind of protest in your hometown. Writing letters to the president or to your congressional representative or senator is another way to let those in power know your views. You might even consider writing a petition for other people who also oppose racial profiling to sign. You can start a petition to the U.S. president at https://petitions.whitehouse.gov.

Texting or tweeting a member of Congress is another good way to make your voice heard. The website http://www.soundoffatcongress.org/ can be useful here. All you have to do is to enter the site, click on Tweet@ Congress, and enter in your ZIP code. You can enter your e-mail, too, but that is optional. Press Continue and, voilà, the site will show your senators and house member. Write your message and send. Encourage others to try it, too.

Protestors hold signs demanding justice for the shooting death of Trayvon Martin in Atlanta, Georgia, on March 26, 2012.

CHAPTER 7

TIMES ARE CHANGING

There are signs of improvement on the racial profiling front. Police departments are training officers to do their jobs with less profiling. There is more action on the governmental front, too. Awareness of the problem is growing. There is reason to hope that racial profiling will some-day be a thing of the past!

FEDERAL SUIT FIGHTS FLORIDA OUTRAGE

Many people have suffered through being racially profiled. But few have gone through an ordeal as extreme as Earl Sampson of Miami Gardens, Florida. As the *New York Daily News* reported, "In the last four years Earl Sampson, 28, has been questioned by police 258 times, searched more than 100 times, jailed 56 times, and arrested for trespassing 62 times. The majority of these citations occurred at his place of work, a Miami Gardens convenience store where the owner says police are racially profiling." Sampson was arrested at least once a week while he was taking out the trash, stocking shelves, or filling the coolers in the back of

207 Quickstop. Luckily, Alex Saleh, his Palestinian American boss, got sick of the way the police treated Sampson and his African American customers and had cameras installed. They showed hundreds of hours of police abuse. As the paper reported:

> "They ask him, "What are you doing here?""
> recalled Saleh. "He said, 'I work here.' The clerk
> said he works here. I said, 'I'm the owner, let him
> go. I work here.' The officer said, 'Yeah right.'

> "So he has more power than me!"

Not only was there video showing Sampson being pushed against the wall and being yanked by an officer while taking garbage out, but Saleh also accuses the police of searching throughout his store without a warrant. Saleh said that the police roughed up many of his customers as well.

For several years, this abuse went unchecked. But finally, a federal civil suit was filed. Now, the city's police chief has retired, and Earl Sampson is on his way to getting a little bit of justice.

THE END OF STOP-AND-FRISK

For ten years, New York City had a controversial "stop, question, and frisk" policy, or, as it was more popularly known, "stop-and-frisk." Under this policy, police were allowed to stop anyone and, with little justification, frisk them.

This policy left a bad taste in the mouths of many of the city's residents of color. According to the *New York Times*, the arrest rate after frisking individuals averaged only 6 percent. That means that for every six people that the police found a reason to arrest, there were also ninety-four other people subjected to humiliating treatment, such as harsh questioning, being publically frisked, being handcuffed, being thrown against police cars, having their belongings searched, and other invasive acts, even though they were totally innocent of any crime. The vast majority

In June 2012, Reverend Al Sharpton (*center, holding sign*) walked with thousands along Fifth Avenue during a silent march to end the "stop-and-frisk" program in New York.

of these citizens were African American or Hispanic. It became hard for any African American not to feel anxious if a police cruiser rolled by.

The mayor of New York defended the policy, saying that it lowered the crime rate. Some people said it was necessary to protect the public, including the African American and Hispanic communities. After all, those groups were also the largest victims of crime, proportionally speaking. According to the White House, black and Hispanic young men make up almost half of the murder victims in the United States each year. They are more than six times as likely to be victims of murder than young white men.

The stop-and-frisk program in New York was ended in the autumn of 2013. After the program ended, police profiled 86 percent fewer people between October and December than they had in those same months of 2012. The percentage of those they arrested went up to 16 percent. Were New Yorkers less safe? No. Murders went down 21 percent in that same time period.

RESTORATIVE JUSTICE

Some schools are avoiding harsh punishments and instead trying an approach called "restorative justice." Many students who live in more impoverished neighborhoods have suffered trauma in their lifetimes. The *New York Times* wrote about Ralph J. Bunche High School in Oakland, California, where students had gone through such serious life-altering events as racial

These educators met in Oakland, California, in March 2013 to study restorative justice, a practice that can help cut down on the tensions caused by racial profiling.

profiling, the murder of friends, the arrests of their parents, and living in foster homes. With no place to express the sadness of these traumas, tensions ran high at the school. Sometimes students got into fights with each other or became defiant or bitter. Before the restorative justice program began, students were also being suspended for such minor infractions as texting. According to the article,

> Among the lost youngsters was Damon Smith, now an A student at Bunche, who said he had been suspended more than fifteen times. "You start thinking it's cool," he said. "You think you're going to come back to school and catch up, but unless you're a genius you won't. It made me want to mess up even more."

> Damon, eighteen, said restorative justice sessions helped him view his behavior through a different lens. "I didn't know how to express emotions with my mouth. I knew how to hit people," he said. "I feel I can go to someone now."

Restorative justice programs try to stop violence and other problems by helping teachers, students, and administrators become closer and more honest with each other. One of the techniques it uses is circle practice. That means students gather with a facilitator and talk openly about the troubles they face. They are allowed to speak without being interrupted.

The U.S. government is even getting in on the act, recognizing that harsh punishments may be backfiring in terms of helping to build a more civil and productive society that works to the benefit of all its people. In 2014, President Barack Obama announced the My Brother's Keeper initiative (http://www.whitehouse .gov/my-brothers-keeper). The initiative's goal is to stop the school-to-prison pipeline for young men and boys of color around the country. The program works with nonprofits and businesses across the country to help keep kids in school and out of the justice system.

One of the reasons that the president wants to involve businesses is because people of color often live in poorer neighborhoods with few job opportunities. If they can get a chance for a job or an internship, it can give them a sense of purpose and hope. Students with a productive goal are more likely to stay in school.

MY BROTHER'S KEEPER

Frequently, students cry—often together—as they recount some of the hardships they have faced.

Part of the restoration process involves undoing harm that one student may have done to another. It involves having the wrongdoer apologize and then take action to make up for what he or she has done. Not every student who gets in a fight is ready to take the steps to redress the wrong he or she has done, but many do. When they do, it builds a greater feeling of trust and

All Americans can work to help make Martin Luther King Jr.'s dream a reality.

empathy among all the participants. And that helps students build a closer, more trusting relationship with the school as well—something that is unlikely to happen if they are suspended or expelled.

Instead of imprisoning someone for a minor crime, the person has to make restitution to the victim. This means making up for the wrong that he or she did. If someone stole something, for instance, he or she may need to do work for the person to pay for what was stolen. The person who stole needs to feel remorse and to understand why what he or she did was wrong. To learn more, check out Restorative Justice International (RJI) (http://restorativejusticeinternational.U.S.).

Progress is coming slowly, but one day, we may come to the day that Reverend Martin Luther King Jr. prophesied when he said, "I look to a day when people will not be judged by the color of their skin, but by the content of their character."

GLOSSARY

arraign Call before a court in order to hear the charges against a person.

arrest To seize a person and take him or her into police custody or control.

bond card A card that police may be willing to accept instead of a driver's license as a way to guarantee that the person will pay for a speeding or other type of ticket.

colorblind Not registering racial differences.

discrimination Unjust treatment of an individual or a group based on prejudice.

ethnic Relating to a group of people having a common national or cultural tradition.

expulsion When a student is kicked out of school as a punishment.

expunge To remove something, such as the record of a criminal charge, from a person's record.

harass To annoy, disturb, and pick on someone.

Hispanic Referring to people who come from a country where Spanish is the national language.

intolerance An unwillingness to recognize and respect differences in other people's views and beliefs.

post-traumatic stress disorder (PTSD) A condition caused by an extremely stressful event that can cause its victims to have flashbacks, sleeplessness, and other symptoms.

prejudice Judging others based on things such as their race, ethnicity, or nationality.

probable cause When police suspect a person may have committed a crime.

racial profiling A practice in which government agents such as the police and judges treat members of minorities on the basis of their race.

racism A belief that people of different races are inferior; this belief may accompany unfair treatment of people who belong to other racial groups.

reasonable suspicion The suspicion by the police that a person is about to commit a crime.

resilience The ability to bounce back from a traumatic event.

rumination Thinking negative thoughts over and over again in a loop.

suspension When a student is forbidden to go to school for a period of time as a punishment.

trigger To cause someone to feel extreme emotions such as rage or depression.

zero tolerance Having to do with policies that make tough punishments for even minor offenses.

FOR MORE INFORMATION

Advancement Project
1220 L Street NW, Suite 850
Washington, DC 20005
(202) 728-9557
Website: http://www.advancementproject.org

The Advancement Project's purpose is to "tackle inequality" on a number of fronts. Along with several resources and links, its website gives information about many of its campaigns, including its important Ending the Schoolhouse to Jailhouse Track. It has information on this project for students, parents, educators, and law enforcement officers, and provides ways to be activists.

American Civil Liberties Union (ACLU)
125 Broad Street, 18th Floor
New York, NY 10004
(212) 549-2500
Website: http://www.aclu.org

The ACLU has a long history of defending civil rights in the courts. Visitors to the organization's website can find updates on many ACLU cases and projects by following the Racial Justice link. There are also links to other legal and justice-related information, including the Bust Card that people can use to remind themselves of their civil rights.

American Immigration Council
1331 G Street NW, Suite 200

Washington, DC 20005
(202) 507-7500
Website: http://www.americanimmigrationcouncil.org

The mission of the American Immigration Council is to strengthen America by honoring its immigrant history and shaping how Americans think and act toward immigration now and in the future. It has a creative writing contest, Youth Achievement Awards, a Legal Action Center, a blog, and ways to get involved.

Amnesty International USA

5 Penn Plaza
New York, NY 10001
(212) 633-4254
Website: http://www.amnestyusa.org

Amnesty USA works to expose and present human rights abuses, both in the United States and around the world. The group has an Immigrants' Rights Are Human Rights campaign. Another campaign is to end police brutality in jails and prisons. Each year the group makes an annual report about the state of human rights in the United States. It has a blog and many ways to get involved.

Canadian Anti-racism Education and Research Society (CAERS)

210-124 East Pender Street
Vancouver, BC V3T 4E3
Canada
(604) 687-7350
Website: http://www.stopracism.ca

This group is dedicated to fighting racism and other forms of hatred. Its website provides a way to report hate crimes and has a number of campaigns, resources, news about different human rights events, an extensive list of definitions of different forms of racism, and resources such as antiracist videos and brochures.

Canadian Race Relations Foundation (CRR)
4576 Yonge Steet, Suite 701
Toronto, ON M2N 6N4
Canada
Website: http://www.crr.ca

The Canadian Race Relations Foundation is a clearinghouse for information about how to fight bigotry in many forms—racism, religious intolerance, and the mistreatment of immigrants—in order to make Canada a more just nation. The organization's website contains an extensive glossary, a library of articles on many topics, resources, information about programs, and initiatives about all kinds of racial problems.

Islamic Networks Group (ING)
3031 Tisch Way, Suite 950
San Jose, CA 95128
(408) 296-7312
Website: http://www.ing.org

This group supports cultural diversity, encourages tolerance, and promotes antibullying. Its website includes a speakers' bureau and curriculum that helps readers gain a greater understanding of the Islamic world.

The Leadership Conference on Civil and Human Rights
1629 K Street NW, 10th Floor

Washington, DC 20006
(202) 466-3311
Website: http://www.civilrights.org

The Leadership Council, founded in 1950, is a coalition of two hundred different organizations that work to advance the civil and human rights of all people in the United States. It tackles several issues, including workers' rights, women's rights, hate crimes, LGBT rights, and racial profiling.

National Association for the Advancement of Colored People (NAACP)

4805 Mt. Hope Drive
Baltimore, MD 21215
(877) 622-2798
Website: http://www.naacp.org

The NAACP was founded in 1909 to fight racism and ensure the equality of all Americans. It works on a number of issues, including health, media diversity, justice, the law, and more. It offers scholarships, a blog, events, ways to take action, and more.

OneAmerica

1225 S. Weller Street, Suite 430
Seattle, WA 98144
(206) 723-2203
Website: https://www.weareoneamerica.org

OneAmerica's mission is to "advance the fundamental principles of democracy and justice through building power in immigrant communities." The group was formed as Hate Free Zone in the aftermath of the September 11, 2001, terrorist attacks to address the backlash on immigrant communities from the Middle East, East Africa, and South Asia that those attacks inspired.

Southern Poverty Law Center (SPLC)
400 Washington Avenue
Montgomery, AL 36104
(334) 956-8200
Website: http://www.splcenter.org

The Southern Poverty Law Center is a nonprofit civil rights organization dedicated to seeking justice and fighting hate and bigotry. The organization gathers information about hate groups in the United States. It issues reports and files lawsuits against groups that seek to oppress the rights of minority groups. Its extensive Teaching Tolerance section creates free books, lesson, plans, documentaries, and other materials to promote tolerance in schools.

WEBSITES

Because of the changing nature of Internet links, Rosen Publishing has developed an online list of websites related to the subject of this book. This site is updated regularly. Please use this link to access the list:

http://www.rosenlinks.com/411/Raci

FOR FURTHER READING

Alexander, Michelle. *The New Jim Crow: Mass Incarceration in the Age of Colorblindness*. New York, NY: The New Press, 2012.

Barlow, David E., and Melissa Hickman Barlow. *Police in a Multicultural Society: An American Story*. New York, NY: Rowman & Littlefield Publishers, 2009.

Bergman, Paul, and Sara J. Berman. *The Criminal Law Handbook: Know Your Rights, Survive the System*. Berkeley, CA: Nolo, 2013.

Brimner, Larry Dane. *Black & White: The Confrontation Between Reverend Fred L. Shuttlesworth and Eugene "Bull" Connor*. Honesdale, PA: Calkins Creek, 2011.

Bryfonski, Dedria. *Islamophobia* (Current Controversies). Farmington Hills, MI: Greenhaven Press, 2012.

Burrell, Tom. *Brainwashed: Challenging the Myth of Black Inferiority*. New York, NY: SmileyBooks, 2010.

Du Bois, W. E. B. *The Souls of Black Folk*. Mineola, NY: Dover Thrift Editions, 1994.

Garvey, Marcus. *Selected Writings and Speeches of Marcus Garvey*. Mineola, NY: Dover Thrift Editions, 2005.

Glover, Karen S. *Racial Profiling: Research, Racism, and Resistance*. Lanham, MD: Rowman & Littlefield Publishers, 2009.

Hahn, Kathy. *Racial Profiling* (At Issue). Farmington Hills, MI: Greenhaven Press, 2010.

Harper, Hill. *Letters to a Young Brother: MANifest Your Destiny*. New York, NY: Penguin, 2007.

Haugen, David, Susan Musser, and Kacy Lovelace, eds. *Should the US Close Its Borders?* (At Issue). Farmington Hills, MI: Greenhaven Press, 2010.

Levinson, Cynthia. *We've Got a Job: The 1963 Birmingham Children's March*. 3rd ed. Atlanta, GA: Peachtree Publishers, 2012.

Marcovitz, Hal. *How Should America Respond to Illegal Immigration?* (In Controversy). San Diego, CA: ReferencePoint Press, 2012.

Mauer, Marc, and Sabrina Jones. *Race to Incarcerate: A Graphic Retelling*. New York, NY: The New Press, 2013.

Merino, Noël, ed. *What Rights Should Illegal Immigrants Have?* (At Issue). Farmington Hills, MI: Greenhaven Press, 2010.

Orr, Tamra. *Racial Profiling* (Essential Viewpoints). Minneapolis, MN: ABDO Group, 2009.

Palmer, Libbi. *The PTSD Workbook for Teens: Simple, Effective Skills for Healing Traumas*. Oakland, CA: New Harbinger Publications, 2012.

Partridge, Elizabeth. *Marching for Freedom: Walk Together, Children, and Don't You Grow Weary*. New York, NY: Viking. 2009.

Thomas, Bonnie. *Creative Expression Activities for Teens: Exploring Identity through Art, Craft and Journaling*. Philadelphia, PA: Jessica Kingsley Publishers, 2011.

Sterling, Terry Green. *Illegal: Life and Death in Arizona's Immigration War Zone*. Guildford, CT: Lyons Press, 2010.

Zinn, Howard, adapted by Rebecca Stefoff. *A Young Person's History of the United States*. New York, NY: Seven Stories Press, 2009.

BIBLIOGRAPHY

ACLU. "New ACLU Report Finds Overwhelming Racial Bias in Marijuana Arrests." American Civil Liberties Union, June 4, 2013. Retrieved February 22, 2014 (https://www.aclu.org/criminal-law -reform/new-aclu-report-finds-overwhelming -racial-bias-marijuana-arrests).

Associated Press. "Racial Profiling in Vermont." *Brattleboro Reformer*, February 18, 2012. Retrieved February 7, 2014 (http://www.reformer.com/ reformereditorials/ci_19992621?source=rss).

Brown, Patricia Leigh. "Opening Up, Students Transform a Vicious Circle." *New York Times*, April 3, 2013. Retrieved January 3, 2014 (http://www .nytimes.com/2013/04/04/education/restorative -justice-programs-take-root-in-schools.html?_r=0).

Brown, Tom, and David Adams. "Miami Suburb Sued for Aggressive Police Tactics, Racial Profiling." Reuters, December 3, 2013. Retrieved February 12, 2014 (http://www.reuters.com/article/2013/12/04/ us-usa-florida-lawsuit-idUSBRE9B303F20131204).

Carroll, Susan. "Man Born at Ben Taub Returns After He's Wrongly Deported." *Houston Chronicle*, September 14, 2010. Retrieved February 15, 2014 (http://www.chron.com/news/houston-texas/article/ Man-born-at-Ben-Taub-returns-after-he-s-wrongly -1694617.php).

Civil Rights Project. "'Out of School and Off Track' Reports Detail Disturbing and Increased Use of Suspensions." UCLA, April 08, 2013. Retrieved February 18, 2014 (http://civilrightsproject.ucla .edu/news/press-releases/2013-press-releases/out -of-school-and-off-track-reports-detail -disturbing-and-increased-use-of-suspensions).

Cose, Ellis. *The End of Anger: A New Generation's Take on Race and Rage.* New York, NY: Harper Collins, 2011.

Fallows, James. "Flying While Half-Arab (and Half-Jewish): This One Is Shocking" *Atlantic,* September 12, 2011. Retrieved May 29, 2014 (http://www.theatlantic.com/national/ archive/2011/09/flying-while-half-arab-and-half- jewish-this-one-is-shocking/244984).

Fellner, Jamie. "Race, Drugs and Law Enforcement in the United States." *Stanford Law and Policy Review,* June 19, 2009. Retrieved February 7, 2014 (http://www.hrw.org/news/2009/06/19/ race-drugs-and-law-enforcement-united-states).

Golgowski, Nina. "Florida Police Accused of Racial Profiling After Stopping Man 258 Times, Charging Him with Trespassing." *New York Daily News,* November 22, 2013. Retrieved February 5, 2014 (http://www.nydailynews.com/news/national/police- stop-man-258-times-charge-trespassing -work-article-1.1526422#ixzz2vi1lANSZ).

Greenwell, Ava. "Helpless as My Son, 13, Was Profiled, Cuffed." CNN, September 21, 2012. Retrieved

February 6, 2014 (http://www.cnn.com/2012/09/21/
opinion/greenwell-son-profiling).

Hawkins-Gaar, Katie, and Alan Duke. "Hollywood
Couple Stopped by Police, Say They Were Racially
Profiled." CNN, October 1, 2013. Retrieved
February 8, 2014 (http://www.cnn.com/2013/09/30/
showbiz/cherie-johnson-dennis-white-police-irpt).

Kunjufu, Jawanza. *Raising Black Boys*. Chicago, IL:
African American Images, 2007.

Lewis, Errol. "America Isn't Colorblind: We Need to
Talk About Racism." *Daily Beast*, July 16, 2013.
Retrieved May 28, 2014 (http://www.thedailybeast.
com/articles/2013/07/16/america-isn-t-colorblind-
we-need-to-talk-about-racism.html).

Maloney, Kevin. "How the George Zimmerman
Case Brought Racial Profiling to the Forefront."
PolicyMic, July 22, 2013. Retrieved February 10,
2014 (http://www.policymic.com/articles/55833/
how-the-george-zimmerman-case-brought-racial
-profiling-to-the-forefront).

National Motorists Organization. "The Realities of
Racial Profiling." Retrieved March 1, 2014 (http://
www.motorists.org/other/racial-profiling).

Postal, Leslie, and Lauren Roth. "Thousands of Student
Arrests Alarm Florida Justice Leaders." *Orlando
Sentinel*, February 10, 2013. Retrieved May 29,
2014 (http://articles.orlandosentinel.com/2013-02
-10/features/os-school-arrests-florida-prison
-pipeline-20130209_1_school-arrests-disabled
-students-juvenile-justice).

Szalavitz, Maia. "Portugal's Drug Experience: New
    Study Confirms Decriminalization Was a Success."
    Time, November 23, 2010. Retrieved February
    9, 2014 (http://healthland.time.com/2010/11/23/
    portugals-drug-experience-new-study-confirms
    -decriminalization-was-a-succes).
University of Chicago. "Social Media Powers Youth
    Participation in Politics." *ScienceDaily*, June 26,
    2012. Retrieved May 29, 2014 (www.sciencedaily
    .com/releases/2012/06/120626121043.htm).
Weiser, Benjamin, and Joseph Goldstein. "Mayor
    Says New York City Will Settle Suits on Stop-
    and-Frisk Tactics." *New York Times*, January 31,
    2014. Retrieved May 29, 2014 (http://www
    .nytimes.com/2014/01/31/nyregion/de-blasio
    -stop-and-frisk.html).

INDEX

ABOUT THE AUTHOR

Alexandra Hanson-Harding has been writing for young people for most of her career. One of her specialties is writing about how young people can empower themselves and find justice in challenging situations. She is the author of twenty books about subjects that include coping with grief, bullying, and activism for girls. She has worked as an editor for such publishers as the Children's Express News Service, Scholastic, MacMillan/McGraw-Hill, and the Rosen Publishing Group. She has written more than one-hundred articles and created educational materials for a variety of other publishers as well.

PHOTO CREDITS